*UN*interrupted

Happiness

The blueprint for relationship success

UNinterrupted Happiness
Copyright © 2019
Phill Andrews, Michelle Farmer Andrews

ISBN: 9781088521052

Table of Contents

Acknowledgements

Thanks to all of you that treasure your relationship and have taken the time and effort to create and maintain a happy relationship. We are grateful for those who weren't afraid to grow through the good, the bad, and the ugly to get peace and Uninterrupted Happiness.

Thank you Jacqueline Escalante Deas, our Sister, friend, and best-selling author. We have always admired you. Thank you for standing in the gap for us and constantly encouraging us to share our tests and testimonies to create the Andrews Blueprint to 30 years of UNinterrupted Happiness. We are so grateful!

Joe and Camille, thanks for being a part of our village and allowing us to be a part of yours. We appreciate your contribution!

Thank you family and friends who have laughed and cried with us, and supported and celebrated our marriage and milestones over the years.

Thank you Mary Kay Ash, the MK family, friends and mentors who were a part of my life and success. You taught me in my early 20's how to help women look and feel beautiful and feel good about themselves while experiencing life transformations.

FOREWORD

By Jacqueline Escalante Deas

Relationships are your greatest asset! When you find someone who values relationships as much as you do, you have found a jewel.

Phill and Michelle are jewels. They have spent years improving the quality of life for others. I've had the opportunity to watch both Phill and Michelle in action as they mentored, coached, brainstormed, and transformed individuals and couples. Not only have I watched them grow other people, I've witnessed growth in my life. They have improved the quality of my relationship with myself and my husband.

I've watched Phill's *straight-to-the-point style* in his business deals and communications. I've seen him make stuff happen. I've seen the homes that he's transformed as well as people that he's empowered. I've seen the before and after lifestyle and reality of men that he's mentored. They evolved from a mundane and unfruitful life to being passionate, wholesome, responsible, and wealthy businessmen. He's a true make-over specialist.

Michelle has literally talked women off the ledge! She's helped them recover and discover themselves. She's a powerful force and presence. She too, has literally changed my life! She is bold, spirited, insightful and intentional. She has a way of adding glamour and sparkle to your life!

Phill and Michelle together are a powerful combination of sunshine, rain, lightning and thunder! Their relationship is a model of success. I've seen them in their happy spaces as well as their low places. They've consistently managed and remained dedicated to their relationship and the well-being of each other. They make each other THE priority and they do it willingly and happily. I've seen them set boundaries and stand firm when others have tried to penetrate their joy and solidarity. They are an intentional strong unit that practices what they preach. I'm grateful that they decided to also preach (share) what they practice. This blueprint that they are sharing will change you and help you create UNinterrupted Happiness. I have learned that happiness doesn't just happen. It has to be created. They will show you how!

This book provides a common sense approach to healing yourself and your relationship. Open your heart, mind and spirit as you begin this journey. Be thankful that this book has landed into your life! You'll find that it is food for your soul and spirit.

As a behavioral professional, I realize that some couples will never commit to marriage or couples therapy, even if they are in crisis. So, this book serves as a way to water the dry areas, shine light on your darkness, provide thunder and strength to areas of weakness, and inject power to the places where you feel low. Embrace the journey to UNinterrupted Happiness!

I. THE BLUEPRINT

The successful completion of anything requires a blueprint. A relationship is no different.

Frequently Asked Questions (FAQ's)

- Why are couples divorcing at such alarming rates?
- Why do I need a blueprint for my relationship?

Millions of books, movies, and songs have been written and produced about relationships. Relationships are at the helm of everything you do! You entered this world as a result of a relationship. The management and maintenance of the core areas of your life such as finances, spirituality, career, health, and recreation all require a relationship with someone. We know that relationships are important, but our success in life depends on our ability to manage these relationships.

The nucleus of every fairy tale is the wish and pursuit of a blissful relationship with a *happily ever after* ending. Think about Cinderella, Snow White, the Seven Dwarfs and the Princess and the Frog. You are no different than they are. All of us, at least the majority of us, are driven by that same desire.

The truth is this -- relationships will always be your greatest asset in your life. Like Cinderella, many have fantasies about starting a blissful relationship, but they don't know how to make it happen. Fortunately, the writers of fairy tales were able to manipulate the outcomes because they produced the tale. They created the ending. What can you do to produce your own fairy tale and happy ending?

Often the problem isn't in the creation of the fairy tales. Sometimes the problem or challenge lies in finding a blueprint to maintain the magic. We have noticed that many couples, whether married or single, have the love but are missing a blueprint that will help them build a strong relationship.

Marriages and relationships are usually made of great people - that's without question. But, just because the people are great, does not mean that the blueprint they have is functional. We have seen a lot of talented, successful and good people walk away from a meaningful relationship. They wanted the relationship to work, but somehow they felt that they did not have the tools to make the relationship work. Consequently, they became a part of the statistic.

Alarming Statistics

The alarming statistics about marriage and relationships confirm that there is a missing ingredient in relationships. Though marriage is a common experience in our culture, divorce is just as common. Many young adults have goals to complete school, find a career, get married, and have children. A lasting marriage is a dream for the ones who marry. But then, something happens.

Approximately, 40 to 50 percent of married couples in the United States get divorced. The divorce rate for subsequent marriages is even higher. If you do an internet search or speak with a Marriage Therapist about the divorce rate, you will hear the 50 percent statistic. *Approximately half of the marriages in the United States will end in divorce.* These statistics are overwhelming.

What are the reasons that couples are divorcing at such an alarming rate? In today's culture, older couples (over 50) are also divorcing at higher rates. According to Psychology Today, the rate of people over 50 who are divorcing, (referred to as Gray divorce) has doubled in less than 30 years.

We explored available research and statistics about the reasons that couples are divorcing. These are the top reasons that marriages fail:

- Infidelity
- Arguing too much
- Lack of commitment
- Domestic violence or abuse
- Substance abuse
- Growing apart

The Need for a Blueprint

These statistics and research beg the questions, "What can I do now so that I don't fall into either of these categories? How can couples get the tools they need to make informed choices before committing to marriage? Suppose married couples had the necessary tools to enrich and protect their relationship?" The ability to produce a great product or a great relationship is based on our access to a functional blueprint and the proper tools. The best chefs have great recipes and the necessary tools to produce their desired outcome. Great builders have the proper tools and resources to create a stunning and well-appointed home.

Can you imagine building a new home without a blueprint? A blueprint is a plan, design or drawing for something that you intend to build. Before a home is built, an architect renders a design and drawing of the floor plan. Every well designed home has a blueprint. Suppose the custom builder who was going to build your home said, "I'm going to start building on Monday and we will just see what happens." You then proceed to say, "We need a blueprint to create the home" and he says, "No, let's just pour the foundation and go with it. We'll build it as we go along." You would immediately fire him! Why should you have faith in him? He has no blueprint or foundation! Without a blueprint he can't build anything. This principle is the same for your relationship. Without a true blueprint, you can't build a lasting relationship. It will start, but it won't last.

Our goal is to help you create a blueprint for your relationship. Whether you desire to get into a relationship or maintain the one that you already have, you will get a blueprint. In this book, we will use the words relationship and home synonymously, quite a bit.

Why Your Relationship is Like a Home

Have you ever gone house shopping and walked in the house and immediately had the thought, "This Is not going to work?" Something about the feel or the floor plan immediately told you that you could never be comfortable there. Perhaps, you couldn't quite put your finger on it, but the feeling alone was enough to suggest that you needed to keep moving.

Relationships are a lot like homes. Think about this; home is a sacred place where you let your guard down and become very vulnerable in every aspect. It's your private place that few people have access to. It is also the place where you hang your heart when it's heavy; express joy freely when you're happy; and let your inhibitions down so that you can be comfortable in your own skin before you go out to the world at large. You want your home to protect you and also reflect who you are. Just as you look for a home that meets your needs, you also want a relationship to meet your needs. Remember, homes and relationships are very similar. Let's be specific about how your home is like a relationship:

- Your home is a protector. It provides security and protects you from outside elements and bad weather, i.e. rain, snow, storms, strong winds, and unbearable heat or cold. A solid relationship will protect you emotionally, spiritually, mentally, socially, physically and financially.

- Your home inspires you. It provides an atmosphere that inspires you spiritually, physically, emotionally, mentally, and socially. It is the place that brings out the best of who you are. Similarly, you want a relationship that is going to accommodate your passions, your present endeavors and goals, as well as your future goals. A solid relationship will inspire you to do and be your best.

- Your home has to be constantly maintained even after you invest in it. The lawn has to be mowed, the interior and exterior will need to be painted occasionally, and repairs will have to be made. When there is a need for a repair, it must be handled immediately so that it does not create more damage. When there is a leak, it will get worse if left unattended. Your relationship has to be maintained and problems must be addressed instead of ignored. Something will always need to be done to improve or maintain the quality of your relationship.

- Your home is a huge investment and will most likely be your largest purchase. Your marriage / significant relationship is a huge investment. When you purchase a home, you consider it an investment and you want the assurance that you are getting good value. No one wants to purchase a home that is a money pit, or a home that has all sorts of major problems. Your relationship / marriage is a huge investment. It can make you or break you.

- Your home has areas that need improvement. The paint color may not be desirable. Perhaps it has some sounds or smells that you don't like. Perhaps, you would prefer different landscaping. Even new homes have nuances that you will have to get used to such as unfamiliar noises, settling, hairline cracks that will eventually happen or a lack of beautiful mature trees. Though those things may not be deal breakers, nevertheless, you are not in denial that they exist. Relationships will also have their strengths and weaknesses. There may be some things aesthetically that you don't like, but can live with.

So, as you are choosing a new relationship, or evaluating your current relationship, it is a good idea to take inventory and ask yourself, "Does my relationship feel like a house or does it feel like home?" There is a difference between the two. A house is a building that you visit which does not necessarily connect with you. You can go in many houses and yet be unmoved by them. A home is a place that embodies who you are; it is a place that you connect with and it connects with you. *It calls you.* Our goal is to help you create or re-create a functional blueprint so that your relationship feels like a home.

Why Us?

We were motivated to write this blueprint because we have 30+ years of success and happiness in our marriage. Yes, we've had trials, adversity, and disappointments just like any other couple. Yet, our happiness has been un-interrupted for the last 30+ years.

Over the last two decades, we have coached individuals, entrepreneurs, and business owners in their relationships. We realized that some of the ingredients that create successful businesses and business relationships also create successful marriages. You must be super intentional with both. As successful business owners, we have crossed the paths of thousands who ache in their relationships, or ache because their relationships ended. As a result of working with so many couples in our businesses, we began coaching couples. We've helped them rebuild their shaky foundations. We've watched them grow and use their new tools to create magic.

The Common Questions

When others discover that we've been happily married for 30 years, they ask a series of questions such as:

- What makes a relationship work successfully and what makes it fail?
- How can I heal myself so that I can transform my relationship?
- How can I prioritize my spouse when there are so many other significant people in my life?
- How do I earn the respect in my relationship, if I have blown it already?
- Why is it so important to set boundaries even with the man or woman that I love so much?
- How do we thrive even though we are so different?
- How can I prevent my past from pooping on my relationship?

Many have asked us to write a book to answer these questions. We felt a special call to share and encourage couples. Here it is! As you take this new journey, remain open, coachable, and available for learning. Be willing to alter your paradigm and throw in your old tools for new and improved ones! We are excited to be a part of your journey!

We will share our tools with you. Though we've been married for 30 years, we still use our blueprint and tools to create magic. We couldn't build by just winging it. We learned that we still needed to be intentional with our fairy tale. Now it's time to create yours. This book will address the following topics and tools:

- Getting your relationship back on track (Ram jacking the foundation)
- Adding the joy, value, magic and excitement back to your relationship
- Managing conflict
- Maintaining and growing your relationship
- Counting the cost and benefits before you jump in
- Becoming an Interior Designer (Redesigning yourself)
- Overcoming pain from the past
- Being a doer
- Creating receipts
- Embracing and committing to change
- Doing Math: 1 +1 = 1
- Understanding roles so that you don't get twisted.
- Understanding you
- The Power of leading and following

Relationship Inventory

I have the power and focus that I need to create the relationship that I desire. This is an opportunity for me to review the current blueprint and make the necessary adjustments. As I move through this journey, I will consider the following questions:

- Did I create this blueprint or was it pre-designed by someone else?

- Are there some changes or adjustments that I need to make on this blueprint?

- Does my relationship have the attributes of a solid home?

2. RAM JACKING: HOW TO REBUILD YOUR FOUNDATION

The way a relationship begins is the way that it is maintained and the way that it ends.

Frequently Asked Questions (FAQ's)

- Is it too late to change the footprint of my relationship even though we've been together for a long time?
- How can I repair a damaged relationship?
- Why do I need a blueprint for my relationship?

Before a home is built, the foundation must be laid correctly. Without a foundation there is no home, no security and absolutely nothing to attach anything of value to. So, from a builder's perspective, the foundation is the most important step in building a home. A foundation is not only important and necessary when building a home, the foundation is also important when building your relationship. The foundation in your relationship refers to the way that your relationship was built. Was it built on trust, honesty, respect, commitment and mutual belief in one another? Or was it built on deception and hostility? In any event, it is important to build a good foundation for the following reasons:

- The foundation creates the structure for everything else in your relationship.
- Your relationship is only as good and strong as your foundation.

Unfortunately, there are times when a foundation becomes weakened or needs to be repaired. As a builder, the main thing that scares potential buyers away from purchasing a home is a faulty foundation.

There are many repairs and changes that a homeowner can do, i.e. painting, installing new floors, laying tile, or changing the landscaping. Foundation repair is costly and requires highly skilled technicians.

Before becoming a builder, I assumed that is was impossible to repair a foundation. After all, the foundation is the bottom and the beginning of the home. Everything else sits on top of the foundation.

Though foundation repair is a big undertaking, I discovered that there is a way and process to fix a foundation. Sometimes the challenge for homebuyers or homeowners is knowing the indicators of a bad foundation.

Ram Jack It

The tell-tale signs of a foundation problem include cracks in the wall, ceiling, or floor; gaps in the door frame and windows; a leaning chimney; and misaligned windows or doors. When a building or home needs foundation work, there are reputable companies that can help repair it. Ram Jack is a well-known, reputable company that specializes in repairing damaged foundations. They come on your site with state of the art equipment and tools to repair your foundation. After evaluating the damage, they will select the best foundation stabilization method for your home. If a home repair specialist or engineer says, "It needs to be Ram jacked," it means that your foundation is in dire need of repair.

Identify the Cracks

As we stated earlier, homes are not the only items that have cracks. Relationships can have cracks that have grown over the years. What do you do when you've been in a relationship for years and cracks have become visibly larger? How do you correct such a problem? Or, is it too late to go back and rebuild a foundation in a relationship? The answer to this question is an absolute "No! It is never too late to rebuild or repair a foundation. However, it must be done carefully and intentionally. And both parties must be willing to repair the cracks and damage.

Before you can rebuild, it is necessary to identify where the cracks are. What and where are the cracks in your relationship? In other words, why was the problem created? Here are some situations that create cracks:

1. Disrespect
2. Abuse
3. Lack of prioritizing your spouse
4. Dishonesty
5. Cheating
6. Mistrust
7. Pain from the past
8. Putting kids before your relationship and not creating proper boundaries for them
9. Lack of communication or poor communication

10. Failure to set rules in the beginning of your relationship

When a couple identifies the cracks in the relationship, it is important to address them. Many couples see the cracks daily, yet continue to overlook them. They assume that the cracks will go away or they assume that the cracks won't get any bigger. Cracks don't disappear by themselves. They have to be repaired. So, when there is a crack in your relationship, it is necessary to create new rules, rituals and feelings in your relationship.

Create New Rules

There are times when you and your partner have the willingness, commitment and desire to repair the foundation. If you are going to repair your relationship, it is necessary to create new rules. Generally speaking, people don't like rules because they believe that rules confine them. Actually, rules set the parameter in your relationship and protect you and your partner. Every relationship needs rules and boundaries. Rules tell your partner where to begin and where and when to end.

If you show me a relationship where anything and everything goes, I will show you a relationship that is filled with misery and disrespect. In other words, you've got to have some rules and a little bit of crazy in you!

Your partner has to know, "I can't just say anything to him or her. I can't just yell at her and get away with it, because she won't be happy."

What new rules do you need to create in your relationship now? Maybe you feel exhausted from cooking and cleaning every day while your partner does nothing. You need new rules, baby! Your new rules might sound like this, "Honey, I will cook three days a week instead of seven days. I am exhausted and can't continue this. What do you suggest that we do the other days so that we share the responsibility?" Your homework assignment is to create new rules.

Create Rituals

In addition to creating new rules, it is important for you to create rituals in a relationship that will be experienced by the two of you alone. Some of these rituals can include praying together, meditating, or walking together. They may include other types of rituals that incorporate your own beliefs and practices. In any event, creating a ritual is extremely important in strengthening the bond of your relationship. One of the rituals that we have created is that of holding each other quietly before we leave the house. During this hold time, we are quiet. As we hug each other quietly, we connect at a higher spiritual level. This connection brings comfort and assurance to us as we depart. It creates a feeling of unity between us.

Create Feelings

A good relationship creates good feelings the majority of the time. Examples of good feelings and emotions are: joy, peace, security, love, trust, forgiveness and excitement. Examples of bad feelings and emotions are: fear, confusion, embarrassment, guilt, shame, regret, resentment, and hatred. While a relationship will experience both good and bad feelings, the goal is to experience more good feelings and to find a way to support each other and bounce back even after experiencing unexpected or undesirable feelings. Here are a few questions to ask yourself:

- What are the dominant feelings and emotions in your relationship?

- When you pull up to your house are you excited to go inside or do you have to sit in the car for a few minutes before you enter?

- Do you greet your spouse when he or she enters the home? Or do you immediately hurry to hug and acknowledge the kids and pets first?

Is It Fix-able?

There may be times when it is necessary to evaluate if foundation repair is in your best interest. Perhaps you've identified the cracks. You have attempted to create new rules, rituals and feelings. However, you do not see any chance of repair. For instance, if you are in an abusive relationship, you will not experience the joy and peace that you deserve. An abusive relationship will break your spirit, rob you of your joy and happiness and may lead to physical harm or death. Abusive relationships are not safe for you or your loved ones.

In instances where there is physical violence, substance abuse, verbal abuse or any other type of abuse, you may have to consider terminating the relationship for your own well-being. There are instances when you may not be able to repair a crack in a relationship. It may create too much risk for you. You must know when it is necessary to move on or out of the relationship. It takes the willingness of both parties to repair the foundation.

Relationship Inventory

The wonderful thing about the power of choice is this -- I get to choose how I enter a relationship. I also have the power to choose to remain in a relationship or terminate a relationship. And I have the option to lay a foundation for my relationship. Sometimes, people allow others to lay the entire foundation and determine the perimeters. I will evaluate our foundation to determine where repairs are needed and then I will proceed to Ram jack the foundation. I will ponder on these questions:

1. Is the foundation in my relationship weak or strong?

2. If it is weak, why is it weak? In other words, how did I participate in creating a weak foundation?

3. If I repair the foundation, what will it cost me? What will be my emotional and mental investment?

4. Is my partner willing to participate in the Ram jack process or can this potentially cause my relationship to end?

5. If the outcome does not create a favorable outcome for both of us, what am I prepared to do?

3. FEED YOUR PLANT: MAINTAINING YOUR RELATIONSHIP

Some say that the grass is always greener on the other side. The truth is, "The grass is greener on the side that you water, the most."

Frequently Asked Questions

- We have great chemistry and get along well. Why is it important to be intentional in maintaining our relationship?
- What can I do to fertilize and grow our relationship?
- What sets some people up for affairs?

Have you ever visited a landscaping nursery? I have always been amazed by the beauty of the flowers and plants there. It feels like an oasis each time I visit. Whenever we purchase a new type of plant, we always ask, "How should we take care of it? We ask the experts because we know that they have a green thumb and are specialists in growing and nurturing plants. The majority of people who plant gardens or have a green thumb, always have a secret about how to get a garden to grow. There are songs that address growing your garden. One nursery rhyme in particular asks the question, "How does your garden grow?" I have heard some say, "Oh, I use Miracle-Gro. I use cow manure." Some say that they use a mixture of soil and peat moss. Certainly, the skilled gardener has a recipe for success and does all that he can to create the perfect garden at home.

Become a Professional Gardener

Good homeowners don't just focus on the home, but on the landscaping around the home. They pay careful attention to the trees, shrubbery, and flowers and plants because they must be constantly maintained. If a garden is going to produce fruit, it needs the right temperature as well as adequate sunshine and water.

Your relationship for all practical purposes is like a garden, which means that you are a Gardener. The savvy gardener studies and researches his plants to learn what they need to thrive. Certain plants need direct sunlight, and then there are other plants that need a little more shade. There are some plants that need to be watered frequently, and then there are others that need to be a little drier. You mission is to figure out how to water your partner's garden. What does he or she need to thrive? Does your partner need lots of compliments or a lot of conversation? Do you notice that your partner acts better, does better, or thinks better when he or she is in a certain environment?

Just as the gardener learns the recipe to grow his / her garden, it is important for you to learn the mix required to grow your own relationship. There are numerous necessities to consider when growing a relationship. Though, it sounds quite complicated, it is nothing short of a plan to constantly grow and improve what matters most to you -- your relationship.

Learn Your Garden

What is your favorite fruit, herb, or vegetable? Have you ever wished that you could grow an abundance of it? When I was a kid I thought the secret to growing anything was to drop a couple of seeds in a cup and add some water to it. I learned that it just doesn't work that way. I soon learned that every vegetable or fruit does not grow the same way and that the process is different for each. Although all plants need water and sunshine to grow, they will need different amounts of water and sun. Some fruits grow better in colder climates, like apples. If you want to grow something, it is necessary to first understand *how* to grow it.

As you think about cultivating your relationship, it is important to thoroughly understand and know the nuances of your partner. Chemistry alone, won't grow a relationship. We had to become intentional with understanding and studying each other. We know what makes each other tick, smile, thrive, and break. Answer these questions as it relates to your partner:

- What makes my partner upset?
- When is my partner happiest?
- What is my partner's personality?
- What environment causes her / him to thrive? *(The beach, the mountains, a clean environment)*
- What are my partner's strengths? What is s(he) absolutely great at?
- What are my partner's weaknesses? What does s/he need to avoid?
- How can I win him / her over?
- What is his / her favorite meal?
- What do I need to do to get favor - take her to her favorite restaurant, cook his favorite dessert, give a massage or back rub?

- What's his / her sexual appetite? What turns him / her on the most?

Grow and Fertilize Your Garden

If you have your own garden, you can simply walk outside and pick your own fruits and vegetables. It's fun and exciting to watch them grow and blossom. After you have taken the time to learn about the fruit or vegetable that you want to grow, you then become intentional with placing it in the right soil and conditions to grow. Miracle-Gro is a popular soil used to help plants, trees and vegetables grow. It is filled with nutrients and food to help plants thrive. Are you and your partner in the right conditions to grow? Do you know how to fertilize your relationship?

The process of producing fruit requires fertilization. It is very important to also fertilize your plant. A fertilizer is a chemical or substance added to your soil to increase the fertility of the plant or flower. Some farmers use cow manure to fertilize their crops. If you ever drive on a country road and smell manure, you know that it's being used as a fertilizer. Fertilizers are messy and smelly, but they are necessary to grow your garden. In other words, growing a relationship requires some work. It's not always convenient and glamorous, but it produces a beautiful, strong, and happy bond.

How to Fertilize Your Garden

There are many ways that you can do to fertilize your relationship. Here are some suggestions to grow your relationship garden:

- *Affirmations.* Affirm your partner. When you choose to affirm someone, you are saying, "I believe in you. You are doing a great job. You are a wonderful wife / husband."

- *Compliments.* Remember, compliments are powerful. Find a reason each day to compliment your partner.

- *Touch.* Everyone needs touch. Some need more touch, hugs, and rubs than others. Know how much your partner needs to thrive and give it to him / her.

- *Warmth.* Create a warm and peaceful climate. Give a smile or wink to your partner.

- *Strengths.* Identify and acknowledge the strengths of your partner.

- *Gratitude.* Show appreciation to your partner for the small things. Don't take kindness for granted.

Avoid the Side Piece!

When couples do not fertilize their relationships, they create a situation for unfavorable results such as anger, divorce, and even infidelity. Affairs shatter relationships. We all know someone who has experienced an affair (or in layman's terms, cheated) in a relationship. We had a dialogue with a colleague who is a professional counselor and trained in Marriage and Family Therapy. She shared this:

Often, affairs start slowly. They don't typically just happen overnight. I recall several situations where couples were having conflicts. In one situation, the husband, Randy felt that his wife, Debbie constantly complained about everything. From the moment he arrived home from work, she began complaining. She complained about the kids, chores, her job, and his lack of help. In an effort to avoid hearing her complain and nag, Randy began to stay at work later. As a result of working more, his stress level increased and he inevitably put himself in a vulnerable situation. One of his colleagues often complimented him about his focus at work and his willingness to be so dedicated. He enjoyed the positive attention and compliments. He felt that someone noticed him and gave him positive feedback. Before long, she became the Side Piece and they began having an affair. The husband said that he fell in the trap because he became vulnerable and hungry for attention.

Randy and Debbie began therapy. Both realized that they should have done things differently. Randy knew that she needed more help at home with the chores and kids. Yet, he gave his all to his job and had nothing left when he came home. He admitted that he was negligent because he did not bother to realize or meet the critical needs in his family. Meanwhile, wife had to come home from work and start dinner, homework and chores. She felt like a single mom. Though she nagged, she was really asking for help. She later realized that she should have used a different approach.

Debbie left the marriage and began having a relationship with someone else. This man did chores and naturally realized when there was a need. Randy did not remain in the relationship that he was in. After Debbie and the kids left the home, he became bitter and angry because he'd lost his family. He said that his family mattered more to him than anything. This situation led to a bitter and painful ending for the couple and the children.

In this circumstance, we see a pattern of neglect, lack of gratitude, and an unwillingness to listen and respond. Unfortunately, some couples do not recover from these adverse situations.

Common Reasons for Extra-Marital Affairs (EMA)

There are several reasons that people give for infidelity. Many assume that couples have extramarital affairs because of sexual boredom. According to research, these are the reasons for infidelity:

- Low self-worth. Sometimes people feel that cheating will improve their self-worth, status, or value. We see this example in "generational cheating." This is a term that I use to describe a long line of cheating, (i.e. the husband cheats on his wife because he saw his Dad cheat on his mother and the Dad cheated because he learned it from his Dad). Somehow they bought into the belief that cheating gains them popularity, a rite of passage or a passing grade.

- Lack of love and excitement (feeling that the relationship is boring and stale).

- Neglect. In the instance of neglect, you feel that you are no longer the priority in your relationship or your partner is no longer your priority.

- Lack of sexual desire. You feel that you have lost sexual interest in your partner or your partner has lost sexual interest in you.

- Lack of emotional intimacy.
- Lack of confidence that the quality of the relationship can be improved.

Tips to Avoid Affairs

In any relationship, you are responsible for your own behavior. We make choices every day. Ultimately, you have to choose to protect your relationship. However, these are some suggestions to help protect the strength of your relationship, as to avoid unnecessary pain.

- **Make Your Partner the Priority!** No one wants to compete with your job, Momma, hobby, baby Momma drama, baby Daddy, or child. Everyone wants to feel like a priority in a relationship. If you have children, it is understood that they have needs and are more dependent on you. However, you do not have to make your partner feel that he / she is an afterthought. Be intentional about how you balance your relationship.

- **Make Quality Time For Your Relationship.** Do you carve out time for your partner or does (s)he have to squeeze in time with you while you are watching television or swiping your phone? The television robs couples of quality time. It is impossible to have quality time with someone while watching television. At that moment, your priority is paying attention to the TV. Don't ever make your partner feel that he has to wait for your favorite TV show to go off before you can listen. This sends the message, "this is more important than you."

- **Un-Bore Yourself.** Sometimes a relationship becomes stagnant and boring after many years. Real examples of boredom that couples complain about are below.

<u>My partner just wants to:</u>

- Watch TV all evening and weekend.
- Talk on the phone non-stop.
- Sit in the house all the time.
- Read books all day.
- Play golf all day, every day.
- Work all day and after hours.
- Play with the kids.

How have you added adventure and excitement to your relationship? If you were courting your partner for the first time, what would you do to add spice to your relationship? Commit to adding some flavor to your relationship. Very few people like bland food or bland relationships.

- **Add Sexual Excitement.** Research proves that men complain more about sex than women do. Men need sex! We are not suggesting that women don't, but men are certainly driven by it. It is often said, "Men give love to get sex, while women give sex to get love." How can you improve your sex life? Are you present while you are making love to your spouse or are you thinking about the kids and work? Bring all of you! Bring a surprise every now and then.

- **Be Emotionally Available and Present.** Women are often accused of being too emotional. Many husbands say that their wives expect them to act like one of the girls. From time to time, women want to be listened to and understood. They want to believe that their partner can empathize with them and understand why they are frustrated, scared, aggressive or passive. They want to feel as if they are "figured out." The truth is, "they can't figure themselves out, sometimes." Men, if you want brownie points, act like you care, check in with them to see how they are feeling about themselves, you, and the world at large. Most women like to talk about *feelings.*

- **Change Your Paradigm About Cheating.** Earlier we addressed *generational* *cheating*. Some people cheat because it's what they saw while growing up. It was the norm in their family. Maybe Dad cheated because he felt that it validated his manhood. It made him popular. Perhaps Mom cheated because it made her feel like she was in control. In any event, it's important to know that infidelity cheapens you and cheats your relationship. It always creates a scar, pain and bitterness. Cheating does not add value to your life. Instead it causes you to lose integrity and synergy with those who respect you such as your partner, children, family and friends.

Synergize

Synergy is the cooperation and commitment of two or more agents (people, organizations, substances, etc.) to produce a combined effect that is greater than the sum of their individual effects. One powerful example of synergy is pollination. I learned that there are some fruit trees that produce best when they are planted alongside a similar tree. For example, plum, apple, and pear trees only produce when they are planted together. When they are planted alongside each other, pollination from one helps the others grow. It is also important for these fruit trees to blossom around the same time so the bees can cross-pollinate them. These fruit trees are technically termed, self-unfruitful because they need another tree for success!

Relationships require the same type of synergy. We function as individuals who are also a unit (or in the box). In essence, the two of you cooperate and collaborate, with the goal of becoming a great unit. In this example, the reality is $1 + 1 = 1$. If someone asked either of us a question individually, we know how the other is going to answer or feel. We have become a strong unit who stands together and protects the other. Check your daily actions, communications, and goals. Make a choice to operate as a unit instead of a lone ranger.

Relationship Inventory

People often say, "The grass is not always greener on the other side of the fence." That is a true statement. I will remember that the grass is greener on the side that I water. As I take a moment to ponder my relationship, I will examine how I am watering my relationship and how I am being watered.

- What am I doing to water my partner on a regular basis? Do I give compliments often and say, "I love you?" I will become intentional with offering help when my partner is overwhelmed. I will ask about the work day and set aside uninterrupted time daily to talk and catch up.

- What does my partner do on a daily basis to grow me?

- Do we have synergy in our relationship?

Assignment: I will ask my partner how I can grow him / her. I will listen and create an atmosphere that fosters honesty. I make a new vow today that I will: never take my partner for granted or assume that she / he will always be with me no matter what I do. I will give my partner respect. I will also build points (receipts) and bring value to our relationship.

4. BECOME AN INTERIOR DESIGNER: WHY YOU MUST DO AN INSIDE JOB

Design is not just what it looks like and feels like. Design is how it works.
Steve Jobs

Frequently Asked Questions

- How does my attitude shape my relationship and determine my results?
- Why is image so important in maintaining a relationship?
- I want to change *how* I show up in this relationship. What can I do differently?

The process of becoming a homeowner is exciting, but it comes with loads of responsibility. After the prospective homeowner selects a home and enters a contract, a professional Home Inspector is hired to evaluate the well-being of the home. The overall purpose is to examine the major systems, (i.e., plumbing, air conditioning, heating, and electrical). The Home Inspector then creates a detailed report which lists all areas that need to be addressed inside and outside of the home. At this point, the prospective buyer and seller focus on the items that must be addressed to close the deal.

By the time the homeowner moves into the home, he/she has identified the areas that need to be changed inside the home such as the paint color, flooring and lighting. The homeowner then quickly moves into *interior design mode.* This process may include several trips to Home Depot, Lowes, or your local home improvement store.

Interior designers are skilled in transforming living spaces and making them functional, safe and beautiful. HGTV constantly features episodes with Interior Designers doing a home makeover. These talented designers also decorate the spaces that they re-design. There is a distinct difference between an interior designer and decorator.

Decorating a space simply requires one to personalize a space by adding accessories, furniture, or changing the color. It is similar to dressing yourself up and putting on beautiful accessories. Designing a space, however, requires a deeper level of work. Examples of designing a space include adding new cabinetry, or changing the flooring or windows. The designer evaluates the current space that he is working with and then creates a plan to change it. Just as designing a home is a detailed process, designing yourself is also a big process.

Becoming the best you, requires an inside job. When you become the best YOU, your relationship will reap the benefits

---

It's an Inside Job

Remember, relationships are a lot like homes! You are also like a home. Just as a home consists of major systems, your body consists of major systems including, but not limited to, the digestive, skeletal, reproductive, respiratory, and excretory (plumbing) systems. Prior to entering a relationship, it is a good idea to do your due diligence and inspect yourself as well as your partner.

Self-inspection requires you to evaluate yourself and identify the changes that are needed internally. Often people have challenges in relationships simply because they do not know who they are. They have not come to know themselves intimately. In other words what we see on the outside of a house and what we see on the inside are two totally different things. Have you ever seen a home that is beautiful on the outside, but a mess inside (holes in the wall, active leaks, mold, damaged flooring, or dirty walls?) There are many people who have this same reality. They are beautiful on the outside and look very functional and well, but are in disrepair internally.

Unfortunately, in relationships a lot of focus is placed on the outside instead of the inside. The curb appeal will get you to the door, but if the home is not tastefully designed on the inside, the interest is lost almost immediately. The bottom line is this - the inside beauty has to be aligned with the outside. It makes no sense to spend thousands of dollars on a roof, paint, brick or landscaping, if the inside of the house is in disarray and disrepair. It makes no sense to dress yourself up, while leaving your negative or sabotaging emotions, thoughts, or attitude unattended. We call this, *"playing dress up."* Sometimes the scars and brokenness from the past or the present have robbed them. So the best gift that you can give yourself and a relationship is that of doing the inside job first.

The Importance of Designing Yourself

I have discovered an important fact - while there are only two people in a marriage or relationship, they bring the baggage, pain, and idiosyncrasies from past relationships and experiences. If you grew up witnessing chaotic relationships all your young life, it will take extra work and learning to understand *how* to create a peaceful relationship. When you experience repeated disappointment, abuse, and adversity, it shapes your mindset and behavior. On the other hand, if your relationships and environment were pleasant, peaceful and encouraging, your perspective may be different from one who has lived a life of chaos, lack, and adversity.

You are blessed to have the opportunity to redesign your life. If you have a design that is currently working against you, it behooves you to release it along with your old mindset, behaviors, thoughts and actions. While you can't change the past, you can recreate your present.

We have spent years doing makeovers on people and homes. I (Michelle) specifically noticed a change in women's behavior when they experienced an inner / outward transformation. Their self-confidence suddenly grew and they left and went out into the world with a totally different attitude! Suppose you did a makeover every day, inside and out?

When you have confidence in yourself, it changes and guides your behavior and thoughts. Confidence causes you to do things that you ordinarily would not do. For instance, you have the courage to build relationships and advocate for yourself. It causes you to welcome new opportunities. When you feel confident, you believe that you are worthy of the best, and you commit to bringing your best YOU to the relationship. What happened? It was a simple redesign.

How to Re-Design Yourself

Your goal is to show up in life with power, purpose, peace and love. If you show up and create your best self, it will inevitably impact your relationships in a positive manner. If you want to redesign yourself so that you can show up with impact, it will require a makeover - a new design. Here are the areas that require interior design:

- Attitude:
- Behavior
- Thoughts
- Speech
- Image

Attitude

Attitude is defined as *the way that you feel and think about something.* Your attitude affects your behavior and it can be your best friend or it can be a weapon that kills, harms, or affects those that it comes in contact with. Unfortunately, I have met women who have bitter attitudes. They are bitter because they've been hurt, disappointed, mistreated and misunderstood. Many of them are still in pain because they either don't know how to get out of pain, or they don't want to let go of the pain. Their past and pain are still bleeding on them. When (if) you have that sort of attitude, it is impossible to maintain a loving and peaceful relationship with anyone, especially a significant other. Here are some questions for you:

- How do you show up in your relationship daily? Are you a pleasure to be around? Are you loving and engaging? Or are you sarcastic and agitated constantly? Does it take a lot of work to be around you?

- If you were someone else, would you want to be in a relationship with you? If you answered, "Yes," that's great news! If you answered, "No", think about what you can do to improve your attitude.

Behavior

Your attitude creates your behavior and actions. For instance, your actions include the way that you and your partner embrace, hug, communicate, handle responsibility, resolve changes and manage disappointments.

What does your behavior and patterns say about you? Do you do what you say you are going to do when you say that you'll do it? If you tell your partner that you will be home at 7 p.m. for dinner, do you come home at 7 or do you handle the commitment lightly and make non-priority stops before you go home? Sometimes the best thought out plans can be interrupted by traffic or unexpected events. However, if you have a pattern of behavior that is undesirable (not following through, making excuses, or not handling responsibility), this is a good time to do some interior design work! Here are some questions to ask yourself about your behavior:

- How do you behave toward your spouse when things are going well?

- What does your behavior look like when you are stressed?

Thoughts

The average person has thousands of thoughts a day. A thought is an invisible, yet powerful idea or suggestion that constantly runs through your mind. Your thoughts become the gateway to good and evil. Many great days are often sabotaged by a thought that you hold. Do you remember the bad dream that you had about your spouse cheating on you or doing something out of character? How did you handle it? If you are like most, you made him (or her) pay for that dream. You had an attitude that wouldn't quit, all because of the thoughts that were created from your dream.

It is important to monitor your thoughts and pay attention to what you think. You are in control of your thoughts and how long you allow your thoughts to entertain you. Random thoughts will constantly try to flirt with you, however, you can choose which thoughts you let into your head. If you notice that you are about to nurse a negative thought, quickly, replace that thought with something positive. Ask yourself the following:

- What are the dominant thoughts that run through my mind?

- Are these thoughts negative or positive? What will I do when a negative thought comes into my mind?

- What are my fears?

Speech

We have all heard the popular bible verse, "Life and death are in the power of the tongue." That is a true statement. You can cause your spouse to come alive with the beautiful, genuine compliments that you give. You can also break your partner down with ugly and demeaning words. I have met beautiful women that lost self - confidence because someone used negative words to break them down. Don't allow others to shoot you with words. You are better than that!

It is equally important to examine the words that you are feeding your spouse. How often do you feed your spouse with positive, loving and comforting words? Words are great assets; they can also be a liability. Answer these questions:

- What are the words that my partner uses to communicate with me? Are these words uplifting or are they negative, mean, and nasty? I have heard people say, "I don't pay attention to those crazy words; they don't hurt me." The truth is -- the words do hurt you. You may not believe it, but your spirit and mind takes it all in and begins to strip you, little by little.

- What words do I choose when I am upset with my spouse? Are my words uplifting or negative?

Image

Your image is worth millions of dollars. Many say, "What's inside is more important than the outside. It's what's inside that really counts." We know that the *inside* is important. But, a good interior designer also knows how to create a beautiful image to woo you! Image refers to the representation or form of something. Your image is the way that you show up physically. It's your look, smell, texture, sound, and movement. The inside of a person is important! We won't disagree with that. But, many times people are drawn into relationships through image. Have you ever seen a man go crazy over a pretty girl who had no brains? It happens all the time.

I know a couple who has gone house-hunting on numerous occasions. The husband says that he will not go inside of a house unless it has the wow factor from the outside. The wife then says, "The inside of the house and the landscaping are equally as important." Husband then says, "Yeah, but if I don't feel good driving up to it, I don't want to deal with the inside of the house. It has to look good before I go inside." His wife then accused him of being superficial. The reality is this - *image is important.* The husband needs curb appeal, while the wife needs the inside and the landscaping to stand out. In any event, image helps us make decisions on a daily basis.

I have seen how couples choose homes over the years. One may tend to minimize the importance of image while to another partner it means just about everything.

The point is this: don't minimize the importance of image. Women, how do you look when you go to bed at night? When you are at home during the day, do you look appetizing, inviting, or are you walking around in those old raggedy pajamas and underwear that you bought 10 years ago? Men, what do you do to woo your partner, do you still look and dress like you are getting ready to go out on a date, do you still wear her favorite cologne or have you gotten so comfortable that you stopped being sexy? When your spouse goes out into the work world, remember, they are bombarded with people who smell and look good. Give your partner a good visual every now and then. Throw away your raggedy undergarments and clothes. Stop walking around inside your home looking like Raggedy Ann or Raggedy Sam!

Relationship Inventory

Today, I will reflect on two areas of my design: my curb appeal and my internal design. I will evaluate my overall image, i.e., my smell, my sound, my physical appearance, and my movements. I will go out of my way to create the *wow factor* in my relationship! I will also remember that I am a reflection of my partner and my partner is a reflection of me. Together, the two of us create a beautiful unit.

- How do I rate my personal appearance (on a scale of 1-5)? What can I do now to improve the way that I look, feel, and smell?

- What are my thoughts, attitude and behavior? What do I need to start or stop doing?

- What does our unit look and feel like?

5. COLLECT RECEIPTS: ADDING VALUE TO YOUR RELATIONSHIP

Always seek to add value to your relationship.

Frequently Asked Questions

- How does a receipt add magic to my relationship?
- What are some ways that I can begin to add value to my relationship?

Collect Receipts

The concept of receipts is powerful in a relationship. When you purchase something (at the store or online) you are given a receipt. The receipt protects you and proves that you indeed made a purchase or investment. If you recall a time when a parent sent you to the store when you were a kid, you probably remember hearing your parent say, "Be sure to get a receipt." Now, as an adult, when I make a purchase, I still have a tendency to get receipts and save them for a while. As a society, we have been conditioned to hold on to receipts.

Receipts are necessary because they provide proof of purchase and allow you to make an exchange or adjustment, if necessary. Certain purchases that you make throughout the year also provide tax advantages. If you perform a service for someone, you make sure that you provide a receipt for record keeping purposes.

In my marriage, I am constantly doing things to add value. There are some things that I do without thinking and then there are things that I do intentionally. For instance, when I make my wife a cup of coffee in the morning, or surprise her with her favorite hot beverage from Starbucks, I have given her something of value. She provides me with a mental receipt. When I whisk her away and take her on an exotic get-away to her favorite island, I get another big receipt. If she cooks my favorite meal, I provide her with a mental receipt. We are always in the process of collecting receipts. Another way to look at this is -- collecting points.

Take a Lesson From Your Favorite Store

Most grocery stores, pharmacies, and department stores, have some sort of points or rewards system for its customers. The more you shop and spend, the more points you collect. Once you collect a certain amount of points, you can use them toward a purchase. If you earn enough frequent flyer miles and points, for instance, you will eventually be entitled to a free flight.

What does a rewards system encourage you to do? It encourages you to do more shopping so that you can keep racking up points. Everyone loves collecting points! It's the same in relationships. But here's the catch; you only get points when you do something positive (add value). You have to be intentional with getting points. When you focus on those points, your relationship will experience more happiness and respect. Let's not forget, the receipt system only works if you have built a strong foundation!

The Value of Receipts

Receipts and points are important in the world of relationships. Receipts build trust and credibility in your relationship. They also create a sense of protection and comfort. When there is a collection of receipts, your partner automatically knows what the outcome is going to be.

Every relationship will have its challenges and bumps in the road. There are times when things are going great and smooth, and then there will be those unavoidable bumps. The receipts or points that you accrued along with way will help you during a time of adversity. Despite the bump in the road, there's a level of confidence because so many points have already been built up. At this point you are still in the green. But when you are going over a bump, and you have no points or receipts, the chances of you working through that situation successfully and gracefully are very, very slim. No points, no wins. If you have not built value in your relationship, your relationship will feel worthless which will result in the relationship ending or continuing in dysfunction.

How to Add Value to Your Relationship

It is never too late to add value to your relationship. At this point, it is a great time to ask yourself the following questions, "Am I adding value to my relationship? How am I adding value? What can I do now to build up receipts?" There are several things that you can begin doing to enhance your relationship.

Check - In

Checking in is the process of asking your partner *how* you are doing in the relationship. You are asking questions such as, "Are you happy with me? Am I in good standing?   What can I do to improve our relationship?"   The check-in process requires total honesty and openness.   The person asking for feedback must be open to whatever is said and the person who is being asked, must be totally truthful.

Strategize

If your goal is to build a strong and happy relationship, it will be important to understand the power of strategy. This means planning your points. Just as an athlete has a strategy to get points for his team, you must have a strategy as well. As you begin to plan your strategy, ask yourself, "What is his favorite restaurant, dessert, or bedroom move? What does she love most -- a back massage, a week-end getaway, a compliment?" Figure out what your partner needs or wants, then give it. This goes back to how you water his or her garden. Once you know, become intentional.

Lay a Brick a Day

You are in a position do something daily to add value to your relationship. The concept of laying brings simply means that you are doing something to build your relationship. Laying bricks does not need to be an enormous task. Examples of laying a brick include making a phone call to say, "Hello, I was just thinking about you and wanted to see how your day is going" or saying "You look great today." If you do those things already, then you are ahead of the game. Other acts of kindness include, packing a lunch with a kind note or giving a foot rub.

How many points have you collected lately? Do you have enough to cash in? Do you have enough points so that you can redeem them later when you hit a bump? Remember to be intentional about adding value to your relationship.

Lead – Follow

There are times when you will lead, and there are times when you will follow. In a relationship, some view "following" as a weakness, while some view "leading" as a strength. The truth is this, at some point, even the strong will follow. Everyone has strengths and weaknesses. People often lead in areas where they feel that they can add the most value. If you don't bring value in any particular area, why should someone follow you? So, be sure to add value.

There are certain things that my wife is naturally good at. She is a good judge of character and she is very observant. If I want some feedback about someone or a situation, I trust my wife's judgment. I am naturally a protector. I wouldn't expect my wife to instinctively handle a safety situation the way that I would.

Understand your strengths and your partner's strengths. Realize that you won't be the boss in every situation! You don't know everything about everything.

Create Happiness

Happiness is a choice. Have you ever been around someone who seems to be happy about everything? They have a natural and contagious appreciation for life. Make a choice that you will do everything you can to experience joy in your relationship. Yes, there are days when you will have challenges and unexpected circumstances that may take the wind out of your sails. Hopefully, those days will be fewer than your happy days. You can have a vested interest in your happiness and your partner's happiness. Do you love to see your partner happy? Does your partner love to see you happy? Commit to happiness. But remember, you are ultimately responsible for your own happiness.

Create Dreams Together

Happy couples have dreams! They still hope and look forward to the future with excitement. They also appreciate the present and realize that they are living the dream. Dreams differ from one season to the next. Take the time to sit down and dream together.

Relationship Inventory

I will become intentional about adding value to my relationship. I will take a moment to reflect on how I have robbed my relationship of value and how I've added value. Everything that I do either adds, diminishes, or maintains the current value.

- Am I adding value on a daily basis? I will check in on a regular basis to evaluate how I am adding or diminishing value.

- What can I do specifically to add value to my relationship over this next week? Here are some examples:

  - Pray for my partner
  - Give a compliment
  - Encourage my partner to do something that he / she has always wanted to do
  - Demonstrate my confidence and faith in her / her abilities
  - Do something romantic that my partner loves
  - Take a short trip so that my partner can get refreshed
  - Cook dinner for a week and relieve my partner of tiresome chores

6. COST - BENEFIT ANALYSIS: HOW TO COUNT THE COSTS AND BENEFITS BEFORE YOU GET IN

Before you build a house, count the cost.

Frequently Asked Questions

- What do I need to know before I get into a new relationship?
- Who has formed my opinion about what a good relationship should look like?

Parents and family often set the expectations for our relationships. From the time we are young children, we hear family members make comments about relationships, what's acceptable and unacceptable or what's attractive and what's not. Did you notice that the women in your family had a tendency to choose men with a certain height, a certain look, or a certain physique? Maybe the men had a tendency to choose women with a certain body shape, eye color, skin color, or hair texture. We become conditioned, often times, to like what our family likes.

People have said that women choose men who are like their fathers while men choose women who are somewhat like their mothers. We allow other people to set the barometer for what we like and what we dislike. This automatically puts us in a false zone for relationships. It sets us up to live and nurture a lie - someone else's lie.

Ask yourself these questions: "What is the package that I am looking for in a significant other? Why am I looking for this type of package? Who told me that this was what I needed to look for?"

Looks Can Be Crooks

Before you enter a relationship it is important to know why you are in that relationship. Are you attracted to that person because you've been taught to be attracted to people with certain physical characteristics? Do you feel that you will have chemistry with a person because of a certain look, smell, height, or color?

I have seen many men in relationships with gorgeous women who look like runway models. They bought into the belief, "if she looks good, then it's all good." But the hell that they went through in the relationship or at home was unbelievable. Some of those beautiful women had bad attitudes, nasty dispositions, and undesirable behavior. Their attitude and emotions did not match their looks. On the flip side, I know women who are in abusive relationships with men who have charisma and the right look. Don't allow appearances to be the major deciding factor when you are considering entering or staying in a relationship. We realize that looks are important, but don't discount the importance of a person's values.

Know Your Values

It is important to choose someone who shares similar values. I just spoke with a friend who is 30 years old, who shared her difficulty with finding someone compatible. I asked her, "Where do you meet your prospects?" She told me that she meets them at the club. I said to her. "Well, there you go! If it's not your intention to remain a *club person*, why would you go to a club to meet a prospective future husband?" I asked her to make a list of the following: activities that she truly enjoys doing, important values, and places that she enjoys visiting.   After she made the list, she discovered that the club was not on her list. It was not a part of her value system. Yet, she felt she needed to visit clubs to find a potential mate.

I truly believe that when you are doing the things that bring joy, you open yourself to meet a person who may be more aligned with you.   He or she may not enjoy every single thing that you enjoy but there will be a mix of some things that you do enjoy.

It's important to understand your value system.   What are your values?   Some value a close-knit family, health and fitness, spirituality, traveling to new places and learning new cultures, and connectedness to friends. So, know your value system so that you can remain true to yourself.   Also, understand the values of the person that you are considering for a relationship.

Before You Say "Yes" to a New Relationship

You owe it to yourself to do the math and count costs before you enter a relationship.   Don't get into a relationship before you do your homework.   Consider the following before you enter a new relationship:

Determine What You Stand For

Don't patronize someone just to be in a relationship. Decide what your non-negotiables are beforehand. If you don't determine what you stand for, you will find yourself dealing with unnecessary headaches and unhappiness. An example of a non-negotiable is: "I will not tolerate abuse of any sort (physical or emotional). I will not marry an addict." You might also add to your list, "I will not get involved with someone who angers easily." You have the right to determine your non-negotiables! This is your life!

Be Open and Bold About Your Non-Negotiables

Don't make someone guess what you stand for. Communicate your non-negotiables upfront. I'm not suggesting that you meet someone on the first date and run through a list. However, if someone does or says something out of character, it is okay to say, "This doesn't work for me." The women who tolerate everything are the ones who are mistreated, abused, and taken for granted. These women create unnecessary pain and hardships for themselves, children, and families. Women are not the only ones who have to be clear about non-negotiables. Men have to be clear as well. Men who don't set ground rules are considered, "pushovers." Some men accept foolishness just so they can have a woman.

There are people who are persistent with communicating their value for the purpose of trying to win your affection. Be careful of the person who is constantly fast-talking and swearing that he is telling the truth. It sometimes can be the offspring of manipulation, also known as "Pimp talk."

Ask Yourself, "Does This Person Make Me Better?"

When you are in a solid and wholesome relationship, you will notice growth in your life. Your life should become better because of your relationship. Ask yourself, "Does this person help me grow personally, professionally, spiritually, financially or emotionally?" If the person does not inspire you to be or do better, you are in the wrong relationship.

Understand Your Likes and Dislikes

It is so important to know who YOU are before you find a partner who is a good fit for you! Many individuals have never taken the time to explore what they really like or dislike. They have spent years accommodating someone else. We refer to these people as Chameleons. Chameleons have the unique ability to blend in so well with its surroundings, it is difficult to identify them. While this ability can be helpful and protect them from predators, it is not so helpful if you have become a chameleon in a relationship. If someone asked you the following questions, what would your answers be?

- What do you enjoy doing? (What are your hobbies?)

- Do you like to travel? If so, where?

- What types of people do you like being around?

- What types of food do you enjoy most?

- What activities do you like, i.e. concerts, clubs, music or outdoor festivals?

- Is church important to you?

- Who is Your Authentic Self?

Understand Your Personality

As you are considering a relationship, it is important to also understand your personality. Are you the fun and free-spirited type or the serious, no-nonsense type? Are you the life of the party or the death of the party? If you are a quiet natured person who is also an introvert, it is important to understand and recognize that. However, if you get into a relationship with a talkative extrovert, you'll need to understand that your partner needs conversation, and your partner will need to understand and respect your need for quietness, every now and then. If you understand your personality, it will help you understand why you do what you do. It also helps you communicate your needs to your partner.

Don't Settle

We have all seen a painful example of someone who has settled in a relationship. When we say, "don't settle" we are really saying, don't accept something or someone that diminishes you. Don't accept someone who does not share your values. Don't say "yes" to something that is not in your best and highest good just because you don't want to be alone. So, don't sell yourself short!

Understand Why You are in the Relationship

Many people have ulterior motives for entering relationships. There are people who are solely looking for someone rich. They are not concerned about the person's character, they just want to live a lavish lifestyle. I've seen women who have endured ass whoopings because they wanted to stay in a relationship with certain comforts. They sold their soul to get material goods. Focus on your happiness and well-being! Don't allow your view of economics to put you in a reckless situation. Be sure that your priority is your happiness!

Relationship Inventory

I will take the time to become intentional about my relationships. Just as I would select a home that is a reflection of my needs, I will consider all aspects of the type of relationship that I desire. I will also get in touch with the "Whys" on this journey. I will explore why I am attracted to a certain kind of person. I will also consider the costs and benefits of my relationship.

What is this relationship costing me? (In other words, what or how am I losing?)
1.
2.
3.

What are the benefits of the relationship that I am in currently? (Or what were the benefits of the previous relationship?)
1.
2.
3.

As I sit and explore my previous relationships, is there a pattern of similar pros and cons?

7. YOU DON'T HAVE TO FIGHT TO WIN

We don't get harmony when everybody sings the same note. Only notes that are different can harmonize. The same is true with people.
Steve Goodier

Frequently Asked Questions

- What creates conflict?
- How can I handle conflict in a graceful and loving manner?

The act of winning does not always happen when you fight. Sometimes, you win by refusing to fight. We often hear others say, "Choose your battles." That statement is very true for relationships. A wise man or woman knows when to engage in battle and how to prevent a battle altogether.

Disagreements and conflict are normal in relationships. There will be times when you agree and he disagrees or vice versa. Disagreements feel uncomfortable because the natural assumption is that a disagreement will lead to a fight or argument. My husband and I can disagree all day long, but it will seldom escalate to an argument. We have learned the art of disagreeing gracefully and lovingly.

The Impact of Conflict

We realize that couples handle conflict differently. But, when there is constant conflict in the relationship, it has an overall negative impact on the relationship and family. There is ample research to support that constant conflict affects the quality and satisfaction of a relationship.

According to research, relationships that are characterized by conflict tend to be less satisfying (Caughlin & Vangelisti, 2006; Fincham & Beach, 1999). Research also supports that conflict in romantic couples was linked to poorer health (e.g., Burman & Margolin, 1992; Kiecolt-Glaser et al, 2005), and identified as a precursor to domestic violence, ineffective parenting, and relationship dissolution (for a review, see Booth, Crouter, & Clements, 2001).

The Impact of Conflict on Children

Research confirms that conflict can also have a negative impact on children (e.g., Amato, Loomis, & Booth, 1995; Jekielek, 1998). In an interview with our colleague, a School Counselor in the public school system, she stated that "children in homes where there is constant conflict, often have difficulty focusing and performing well in school. These children also exhibit higher levels of anxiety and sadness. On many occasions, these students came to school agitated because they had difficulty sleeping the night before."

How Do You Handle Conflict?

Conflicts that are dealt with constructively do not have the same negative effects on relationships as conflicts in which partners engage in negative, relationship-harming behaviors (for a review, see Heyman, 2001). Conflict in a relationship is unavoidable. However, the *way* that you handle conflict can improve the quality of your relationship.

It is not uncommon for individuals to handle conflict the way they saw their parents or loved ones handle conflict. If a parent handled conflict aggressively and cussed out everyone in the house when he / she was upset, it is not uncommon for the child to handle conflict the same way. The child becomes an adult who becomes aggressive and punishes everyone in the home because he / she is upset. We are not suggesting that *everyone* handles conflict the way a parent did, but the way that we handle conflicts is often learned behavior.

When most couples have a disagreement, they are not usually disagreeing to start a fight. Couples often disagree because they are from different backgrounds with different experiences and perspectives. Sometimes the willingness to disagree, simply reflects your comfort with sharing your opinions, thoughts and feelings even though they may differ from your partner's. When you disagree or when there is conflict, how do you handle it? Review the list below. Do you relate to any of these?

- I immediately get family and friends involved in our conflict
- I lose my cool and go in the red zone and everyone in the home becomes afraid
- I become violent
- I leave home (disappear)

- I turn to the bottle (alcohol) or drugs
- I go into silent mode and shut down
- I become verbally abusive and condescending
- I become vindictive and go on a mission to get even

Strategies for Managing Conflict (Battles)

The examples in the section above are just a few of the negative ways that conflict is handled. Have you noticed a pattern in the way that you handle conflict? Do you handle conflict in an effective manner or do you handle it in a way that perpetuates more conflict? How can you handle conflict gracefully so that you don't have to declare a state of emergency in your home? If you are going to return to a place of peace, it is necessary to identify what your conflict is really and create a strategy.

The strategies below will help you understand the reasons that you have conflict and provide some practical ways to manage it.

Determine What the Conflict Really Is About

There are instances when couples are arguing about something that happened in the past. You have to determine *what* the enemy is. Are there a series of unresolved issues that cause the slightest agitation when there is a problem? Is she angry because of how you make her feel when you say or do something? Does he feel disrespected by what you said or did? What emotions are fueling this conflict? Is it fear, guilt, resentment or anger? Is there an outside influence that is fueling the conflict?

Commit to Getting Your Emotions Under Control

You can change the way that you handle conflict. If you practice self-control, your relationships will improve in every area (i.e. romance, work, family, friends.) You must realize and remember that you are in control of your emotions and how you handle a situation. You can't use your crazy behavior or reaction as an excuse. No one wants to hear, "I can't help it. It's just the way I'm wired." Figure out how to disconnect the wires. We expect toddlers to have temper tantrums when they are upset, but we don't expect adults to spin out of control when they don't get their way.

Choose Your Words Wisely

When a person is upset and in a disagreement, he / she may use unnecessary words such as, "*you always or you never.*" When you are experiencing a heated conflict, what words do you fall back on? Do you go in your word arsenal and look for words that stab like a knife? We may not want to physically fight or throw a punch, so we resort to using words that can punch. Words are just as powerful as a punch. Words have memories, feelings, and emotions attached to them. That old adage and childhood chant, "sticks and stones may break my bones, but words will never hurt me" is one of the biggest myths that I've ever heard. Words hurt, long after the issue is resolved. The memory of certain words still linger. Sometimes, it is those words that really diminish the trust in a relationship. What are the words in your word bank?

Determine What's Really Important (or Unimportant)

I once heard an older couple that had been married for years, give this advice: "When you are not getting along or not agreeing about something, ask yourself, "Is this something that will matter when you turn eighty? Will it really make a difference?" That advice put things in perspective for us. There are times when you have to really decide in advance what you are going to become rattled about.

Sources

Burman, B., & Margolin, G. (1992). Analysis of the association between marital relationships and health problems: an interactional perspective. *Psychological bulletin, 112,* 39-63.

Caughlin, J. P., & Vangelisti, A. L. (2006). Conflict in dating and romantic relationships. In J. Oetzel & S. Ting-Toomey (Eds.), *The Sage handbook of conflict communication* (pp. 129-157). Thousand Oaks, CA: Sage.

Fincham, F. D., & Beach, S. R. (1999). Conflict in marriage: Implications for working with couples. *Annual Review of Psychology, 50,* 47-77.

Jekielek S. (1998). Parental conflict, marital disruption and children's emotional well-being. *Social Forces, 76,*905–936.

Heyman, R. E. (2001). Observation of couple conflicts: Clinical assessment applications, stubborn truths, and shaky foundations. *Psychological assessment, 13*(1), 5. Kiecolt-Glaser, J., Loving, T., Stowell, J., Malarkey, W., Lemeshow, S., Dickinson, S., et al. (2005). Hostile marital interactions, proinflammatory cytokine production, and wound healing. *Archives of General Psychiatry, 63,* 1377-1384.

Relationship Inventory

Today, I will take a close look at my relationship and identify how I handle conflict. I can choose to handle it differently if we are not getting results or solving the problem. While I cannot change the behavior of my partner, I can choose and change my own behavior.

- How do I respond to my partner when there is a conflict?

- How does my partner respond to me?

- What effect has the conflict had on my relationship and other relationships?

- How can we work together to manage the chaos or conflict?

8. HEALING OLD WOUNDS: DON'T LET YOUR PAST SABOTAGE YOUR PRESENT

Living in the past is like paying rent for something that you no longer own.

Jacqueline Escalante Deas

Frequently Asked Questions

- How can I recover from the pain from my past?
- I've heard that the success of my relationship is dependent on my willingness to heal. How so?

You are a product of your parents' past – good or bad. This means that you are and will be affected by the past and pains of your parents. Your parents did their best to raise you, but if they were dysfunctional, angry, bitter and hurt - they undoubtedly brought that into their relationship with you. This is the reason that many situations (good or bad) are multi-generational. For instance, it is not uncommon for issues such as teen pregnancy, addictions or dropping out of school to appear in several members of one family. Consequently, in your current relationship, you're not only dealing with your own pain and issues, you are also dealing with the baggage and the pain that your parents have (or had). Sometimes, it is this very pain that has created conflict in your present relationship. For a moment, think about your parents and elders. Do you notice that you have similar beliefs, habits, struggles or successes that they had? When you recognize the commonalities, it puts you in a position of power so that you can begin to heal old wounds.

Heal the Wounds

There are wounds that we experience from our past as a result of the family. There are also new wounds and scars that we collect from other relationships. I (Phill) really had to heal past hurts from a previous betrayal. I was in a marriage that had a rocky middle and ending.

In the beginning of this relationship, I did well financially. I was a wealthy businessman, living well -- *I thought.* Then came the betrayal. This betrayal affected my emotional and physical well-being. Despite the pain, I knew one thing; *I did not want to remain broken and in despair.* I knew that I was going to have to find a way to bounce back.

People often ask, "Phill, how did you heal, bounce back and trust again?" Most men would have stayed angry. Fortunately, I began a path to healing. I learned some valuable lessons on this journey, which I shared, with many men (and continue to share with them).

A Word to Men:

Men, it can be very difficult for us to be vulnerable because we are taught that we should not be vulnerable. We are supposed to be in charge of our emotions and feelings at all times. That is one of the biggest myths. Men, we too, hurt. We get disappointed. There are times when we have to become vulnerable and admit our pain. Think about how long it takes for a man to go to a doctor to remedy a situation that could have been taken care of a long time ago. Think about how long a man must drive around and get lost before he finally decides to ask for directions. We are programmed to lie to others and ourselves. If you are to bring the best to your relationship and become your best self, it requires you to be vulnerable. Vulnerability simply means that you are honest with yourself about your feelings and your mental space. It is also important to be honest with your partner about your pain, scars and fears. The perfect partner for you will be able to handle all of you. Some will walk away after they discover your pain and past. But, there is someone who will love you in your pain because she can see past your pain and accept that you are in a temporary space. Thankfully, my wife saw past my pain because she knew my potential and my patterns.

Men, when you expose your pain, you must also be willing to heal it. A woman wants to see that you are strong enough and willing to heal your pain and move past it. For most women, it's not the pain of your past that they fear – it is the power that the pain will have, if you don't heal it.

You cannot commit to change unless you first admit your need for change.

Admit Your Pain

I had to admit that I was in pain. When I admitted to my pain, I could commit to getting out of pain. Each of us has a past. Many of us impose our past on our wives and significant others. I challenge you to look at your pain, anger and the root of it. Sometimes, your pain may stem from the relationship with your mother, father or grandparent. Sometimes, it may stem from something else. If you find that you get angry and enter the Red Zone easily, or feel the need to fight and defend yourself all the time, chances are you are a victim of your past.

Steps to Healing Old Wounds

Your past does not have to continue bleeding on you now. In other words, your past doesn't have to sabotage your or your relationships. Yes, the injury may have left a scar, but it doesn't have to control you or others. Here are the steps that I took to heal from my personal pain.

Find An Outlet

When you are hurting or dealing with emotions that are consuming you, it is important to find a positive outlet or something that you can do to help balance your emotions. Examples of an outlet include going to the fitness center, running daily, painting, playing golf, shooting pool (billiards), camping, or gardening. Find an outlet that resonates with you. At first, you probably won't feel like focusing on an extracurricular activity. But, you'll soon discover that you will begin to feel and think better as you circulate your energy to something positive.

Tap Into Your Spirituality

It is important to connect to a spiritual source. My intellect, strength, and vision are limited, but God's wisdom and power are limitless. It is my connection with God that has helped me sustain a 30 year marriage with uninterrupted happiness. You might ask, "What is the benefit of relying and trusting God?" God has and continues to provide a map for me to follow in our daily relationship. You will find that you'll constantly need God's wisdom for your business, finances, health and marriage. Fortunately, you do not have to operate in the dark. We did not come into this world alone and we can't exist alone. We must rely on the power of God. I still rely on God's wisdom, strength, and power for my life and marriage.

Work On Yourself

The process of healing requires honesty and vulnerability with yourself and others. Think about this, when you call a contractor to set an appointment for a repair, you must first explain the problem. He then visits your home to diagnose the problem so that he can fix it. Your home is your private oasis. We often don't like to invite strangers into our home. However, when you want something fixed or eliminated, it requires a degree of vulnerability. You are allowing someone to come into your intimate space to fix something. It is the same when working on you. You will find that you cannot heal yourself alone. It requires the assistance of others, i.e., a therapist, coach, trusted friend, or someone who has the expertise to move you from where you are to where you want to go.

We have addressed the important process of working on you. Now is a perfect time to explore "what" needs to be fixed in your life. Ask yourself these questions:

- What is bothering me right now? What is still bothering me from the past?

- What are the feelings that surface when I think about that person or situation?
- How is my current attitude and how does it contribute to my pain?
- What are my perceptions about the pain?

- Do I still see myself as the victim?
- Who have I blamed?

If you were sincere when you answered these questions, it will give you a map of "what" you can work on so that you can begin the healing process.

Completely Exhaust Yourself (via exercise)

Believe it or not, exhaustion has its benefits. When I was healing emotionally, a wise coach told me, "Fatigue yourself so that the real you can surface. I want you to totally exhaust yourself so that your mind is clear." Since I was an athlete, I understood what exhaustion meant. I decided to start running. Running felt great. One day, I ran until my body was completely exhausted and my mind was completely empty. After I exhausted myself, I was too tired to think about the mental pain. I did not have the energy to manipulate my thoughts. When I became too tired to think, Wisdom met me. I began to thoroughly understand the importance of three important actions – exercise, meditation, letting go, and rest.

Research shows that exercise improves your physical and emotional well-being and helps diminish depression and anxiety. Dr. Michael Craig Miller, Assistant Professor of Psychiatry at Harvard Medical School stated that exercise can work as well as antidepressants for some people. According to Dr. Callaghan, (2004) exercise is helpful in improving mental health by reducing anxiety, depression, and negative mood. According to M. Guszkowska (2004), exercise alleviates symptoms such as low self-esteem and social withdrawal.

The Power of Meditation

After beginning a routine of exercise, I began to meditate. I allowed God to impregnate my mind with thoughts of peace, strength, confidence and comfort. My trust and faith in God became stronger. Also, my trust and confidence in myself became stronger. I stopped seeing myself as the victim and committed to letting it all go. I stopped asking myself, "Why did this happen to me? What did I do to create this?" After I started taking responsibility for myself and what happens to me, I was able to let go of the "Why" and rebuild myself. I had to ram jack my foundation. When you continue to see yourself as a victim, you will remain a victim and you will continue to be owned by the predator. I chose to see myself as a Victor! Each day, I carefully chose the words that I spoke and listened too, and the people that I hung around.

Get Your Rest and Sleep!

It seems like common sense to know that rest and sleep are important. Yet, when you are stressed and in pain, it is common to sleep less and forget the importance of resting the mind and body. Your sleep heals you. It gives your body and mind the opportunity to relax and refuel for the next day.   Research and literature provided by the Division of Sleep Medicine at Harvard University, support the following:

- Insufficient sleep may possibly lead to diabetes (Type 2) by influencing the way the body processes glucose.

- A night of inadequate sleep for people with hypertension may cause elevated blood pressure the next day.

- Chronic sleep issues have been associated with depression, anxiety, and mental distress. In one study, the subjects who slept less than 5 hours a night reported that they felt more stressed, sad, angry, and mentally exhausted.

While this book is not about sleep or health issues, it's important to realize the importance of rest and sleep as you are healing. Pain and trauma brings enough mental and emotional distress of its own. When you deprive your body of the rest and sleep that it needs, it perpetuates your problem by also putting you at risk of disease, mental stress and other conditions. So get your rest and go to sleep!

Ask God the Magic Question

My pain drove me to a place of heightened faith, focus and courage. I was so broken that I had no choice but to trust the power and wisdom of God. I knew that I had to trust God as well as myself to love and trust again. Though my trust was shattered, I believed that it was possible to love again. I believed that the next time was going to be different and better. I took a leap of faith and asked God, "Will you please send me someone special who will appreciate me, respect me and believe in me?" Five months later, (July 1982) I met Michelle. She saw my brokenness and my pain, but she also saw my potential and my heart. She somehow knew that beneath the pain was a man who was committed to his growth as well as hers. She saw my drive for success. She allowed me to love her and she allowed herself to love me. But most important, she BELIEVED in me because I gave her reasons to trust and believe. I was different with her. The belief she had in me was empowering. I had someone who was sincerely committed to me and us. As a result of my partnership with her, my new faith in myself, and restored faith in God, I was completely changed from what I once was. I love her so much for her emotional, mental, and spiritual investment in me!

Your circumstance will be different than mine. You will still need answers and guidance. Don't be afraid to ask the magic question. If you want to experience Magic, you have to ask the magic question. After you ask the question, trust that the solution / answer will come. Just be ready for the solution!

Sources

Callaghan P.. Exercise: a neglected intervention in mental health care? Journal of Psychiatric and Mental Health Nursing. 2004;11:476–483.

Guszkowska M.. Effects of exercise on anxiety, depression and mood [in Polish] Psychiatria Pol. 2004;38:611–620.

Division of Sleep Medicine at Harvard Medical School: http://healthysleep.med.harvard.edu/healthy/matters/consequences/sleep-and-disease-risk.

Relationship Inventory

I will be totally honest about my feelings and my pain. I will not deny my feelings. Instead, I will embrace them, the good and the bad. I will give myself permission to be vulnerable, to be in pain, and to acknowledge the pain. Though I am in pain, it does not mean that I have to remain in pain. I will realize that I cannot heal what I am not willing to reveal to myself or even to my partner. Now, I will invest in discovering how to heal so that I can turn my scars into Stars.

Pain is not always visible. Pain can be subtle and hidden. Pain surfaces and shows up as bitterness, being critical and judgmental, feeling the need to defend yourself all the time, not trusting yourself or others, fighting every time you are mad with someone, addiction, constant sarcasm, over eating, over working, or being afraid. I will honestly reflect on the following questions:

- Am I willing to admit that I have some pain?

- How is pain showing up in my personal life?

- How is my pain showing up in my relationships? How has it showed up in past relationships?

- What is my belief about the pain? Do I believe that it will never go away or get better? Have I made excuses for holding on to the pain?

- What am I willing to do now to treat the pain so that I can get rid of it?

- Am I coachable? Or am I a *know it all?* Know it all's never get out of pain because they are too prideful to admit their need for help.

- What am I doing physically to help myself stay healthy (exercising, getting adequate sleep, praying, meditating?)

- What am I saying about my circumstance? Who am I listening to?

9. MANAGING ME, US AND THE KIDS

One of the best things you can do for your marriage and your children is create balance. They will both appreciate it, if not now, later.

Frequently Asked Questions

- How in the world do I balance relationships with my partner and my kids so that I stay sane?
- I have kids. What should I consider before getting into a new relationship with someone?
- What is the importance of boundaries?

In our marriage, we have been blessed to partner with wonderful couples. We've learned from them and leaned on them. Their family has become our family. Several decades ago we met a dynamic couple, Joe and Camille. They have been married for 36 years. We watched them raise three wonderful boys who are now adults. All of these boys are well mannered, well-travelled, college educated, smart, responsible, and successful. They are making great contributions to society.

12 Strategies to a Healthy and Hearty Marriage, While Parenting

We constantly saw the love, respect and admiration that Joe and Camille had (and still have) for each other. We were always inspired by their dedication to each other and their children. We asked them to take their inspiration further and provide practical insight about managing and maintaining a relationship while parenting. They suggest twelve (12) strategies for parenting so that you keep your sanity and your relationship intact!

Set Boundaries

We were married in our early twenties. We had our first child ten months after we wed. We then relocated to Delaware when our boys were 12, 10, and 5. As we began parenting, we realized that we had to be strategic! We put several practices in place to help us grow a healthy relationship and family.

We realized early on that boundaries and balance were important. Every great relationship has boundaries and balance. While some may frown on setting boundaries and creating balance, it will help you maintain peace and happiness in your home! One of the most important suggestions that we give parents is – **have a set bedtime for kids!** This will give you time to decompress, catch your breath, reflect and spend time alone with your partner.

When one parent spends every waking moment catering to children, cleaning, or cooking it is very difficult to have the energy or willingness to be romantic at the end of the evening! If you begin to set boundaries with your children, it will allow you to make and keep each other a priority. Your children will not die if you say, "no" to them.

Over the years, we've always made each other a priority in the midst of constant demands. We had numerous demands with work, two jobs, and extracurricular activities for our kids. Each of our children ran track and played other sports. Amidst the demands and hectic schedule, it was important for us to have peace and harmony in our home. Boundaries saved us!

Create a Village (Support System)

We developed friendships with our neighbors, other parents, and colleagues that we worked with. They could count on us and we could on them. We were open to creating a new family (outside of our biological family). Though we had our own biological family, we knew that we had to expand our definition of family and embrace others as extended family. It is difficult and impossible to raise a child in isolation. One time, both of our kids forgot their keys to get into the house. We were both at work. The neighbors took care of them until we got home from work. When we got home they had been fed and were in the bed. Thankfully, we had created a village that we could trust.

After you create your village, you will realize that your kids need time away from you, too. They need time with their peers. They have to have relationships in order to build their social skills! Create your village.

Develop Trust

It can be difficult to leave your children with others. As a parent, you work hard to protect your children from the unknowns and from others who may not have their best interest at heart. Yet, you can't raise your child in a bubble. When you create a support system, it also requires you to trust the people that you surround your child with. I've heard some parents say, "You can't trust other people. How can I protect my child from pedophiles?" Here are some suggestions:

- Build a relationship with others in your village. Get to know them and do things together for a while to observe their behavior and patterns;

- Be prayerful. Ask for divine guidance, as you are parenting and building relationships with others;

- Have the Talk with your child. Let your child know that no one has the right to touch a private area and no one has the right to ask your child to touch private areas of anyone else. Encourage your child to talk to you if anyone makes him / her feel uncomfortable;

- Take notice of your child's behavior when he returns home from a visit with someone. Is your child happy, sad, or indifferent? Ask questions about the visit.

Create Rituals

What are some rituals that you already have in your home? Can you remember some of the rituals your parents or family created? Did you family eat together daily, have daily prayers, or have family talk time? We always ate dinner together. This was our time to catch up with our sons and find out what was going on in their world. It also gave them the opportunity to find out how we were doing. Consider creating rituals in your family that will help build stronger relationships with one another.

In addition to creating rituals with our sons, we also had a "Date Night" ritual. We became very intentional about planning a night for a date or a weekend getaway. Be sure to become intentional with creating time for you and your partner to be alone.

Be Flexible

In our home, we never imposed traditional duties on each other. We did not expect one to do all the cooking, or the other to do all of the laundry. We chose to fill the needs. One of us was better at managing the finances; the other did more of the cooking. Yet, we did not sit around and wait for the other to do a chore.

One day, I (Joe) was changing my son's diaper. My uncle said, "Man, you change diapers?" I said, "Absolutely. He needs to be changed!" My wife loved that I was an *All Hands on Deck* man. We shared the chores. I did the cooking during the week because I came home first. When I was growing up, my Dad also cooked. Our family was not rigid with chores. We learned how to be flexible.

Ask for Help

There are times in a relationship where one person will over function and the other person will under function. If you are the one who has taken on the majority of the load, it is time to ask yourself an important question, "Why am I over functioning? What do I need help with?" Make a decision to ask your partner for help. You don't have to be a lone ranger, do you? Tell your partner what you need. Be specific and say, "Honey, I need help cleaning after I cook. I will cook dinner, but I would appreciate if you clean the dishes after dinner. That would help out a great deal." Or, if you have kids and you are over functioning, why not say, "Honey, I don't mind getting up 4 nights a week with the baby, it would help out if you can get up on the other nights. I'm exhausted."

Avoid the Superwoman Trap

I (Camille) believe that the way you start a marriage is important. Don't start off doing something that you can't or won't maintain. Don't start off over functioning just because you want to impress someone. This will work to your disadvantage in the future.

Often times, women feel that they have to be all things to all people. We feel that we have to be everything in the home, i.e. the cook, nurse, maid, teacher and the driver. When you over function, you will automatically set someone up to under function. Think about the way you are in your relationship. Are you constantly overworking yourself?

It is important to teach your children to become responsible. As they get older, give them more responsibility for themselves. This will create the time that you can devote to your spouse. As far as resources, give children what you can and what you feel that's appropriate, but be sure to teach them financial principles and responsibilities for some of the things they want.

Be on the Same Page

An issue that often creates conflict in a marriage is the difference in parenting styles. It's important to be united when you are parenting. If a child knows that he can manipulate one parent to get his way, he will certainly do it. On the flip side, if a child knows that when Dad says "No", that Mom will also say, "No" they are less likely to try and manipulate. They have to be taught that both of you are on the same page. Certainly there will be times when you disagree on something involving your child. The child does not have to know that there is a disagreement.

Understand Parenting Styles

It is important to establish how you will communicate and discipline your children. Many of your parenting beliefs and values will be based on "the way" that your parents raised you. What are the consequences when your child does not obey? How many chances will you give her before punishment? What will punishment look like?

Discuss how your parents raised you and determine which rigid issues you want to relax and which lenient issues you want to tighten up. One thing is certain; there is no cookie-cutter way to raise children! They all have different personalities, behaviors and moods and you have to treat them accordingly. The communication style that you use with one child may be very ineffective with another child.

Think Before You Blend

There are more blended families today than there were years ago. A blended family is one in which a partner or both partners bring children into the relationship. Often, couples do not consider how the BLEND will work for / against them. If you have children and you are considering a relationship with someone, ask yourself, "Does this person have my child's best interest at heart?" Pay attention to how your partner communicates with your child and vice versa. If you plan on having children with your partner, be upfront about expectations regarding the current children in the relationship. I've seen situations where the woman has a child and he has none, then when the couple had a child together, the other child was pushed to the side.

Discuss parenting styles with each other. Also discuss the boundaries, standards and rules with the other parents. It will probably work out best if all parents agree upon expectations. If you can't iron this out before you get married, it is an indication that you need to move on.

Know *who* you are marrying. In order to live in the same household peacefully, both parents have to have input and involvement. You have to be on the same page. Remember, if your partner is strongly against you parenting his/her child, it will not be a peaceful relationship.

111

Give Your Children Responsibility

We've known couples who were extremely doting on their children, and required very little of them. Because these children were deprived of responsibility, they become dependent adults. Studies have shown that children who have responsibility become more responsible. Consequently, they have higher self-esteem and they are more confident and self-sufficient.

Model Behavior

Family dynamics play a major role in the behavior of children and adults. Children mimic their parents' and older siblings' behavior (good and bad.) Make sure that you model the behavior that you desire to see. If you want your children to respect adults, they must see you respect your elders. If you disrespect your parents, you send a message to them that it's okay to be disrespectful. If you use good manners, they will also learn the importance of good manners.

Relationship Inventory

I will become intentional with setting boundaries and creating balance because I now realize that it is necessary for my sanity! As a parent, I realize that I set the tone for our home. Though I have children, I will remember to make my spouse a priority because one day, my children will become adults and leave home.

- How have I set boundaries?

- How do I create balance in my life and home?

- Who do I consider a member of my village?

- Do I give my children the opportunity to build relationships with others or have I become a helicopter parent?

- How am I teaching responsibility to my children?

10. THE CONCLUSION

From the beginning of this book, we shared the concepts about belief, building a strong foundation, growing and maintaining your garden, staying in the box, and accumulating receipts. We've used these same concepts and ideas to maintain our Union and produce consistent happiness and fulfillment.

While this book provides great information, the factors that will bring the transformation that you desire are belief and implementation (taking action). Believing in each other is everything! It's the strongest layer of the foundation. Without belief, you have nothing. I have heard many divorcees say, "I still love him or her but the trust and belief have gone. We can be friends but we can't co-exist in the same home. He / she is not the person that I thought he / she was. We've just grown apart." In many instances, these couples stop believing and they stop taking action.

Action is always required if you are going to experience change.The quality and strength in your life are contingent upon your actions, choices and relationships. You are only as powerful as your relationships!

As you continue on this journey, give yourself permission to win and be happy. Surround yourself with people who are already winning. Become committed to winning!

We trust that you have gleaned wisdom and practical strategies that have helped strengthen you and your relationship. Many of the principles in this book will also help transform your other relationships.

Thank you for investing your time in reading our book. We wish you an abundance of success and Uninterrupted Happiness as we have experienced over the last 30 years. We look forward to the next 30 years! Use the concepts and principles in this book to create and experience your own happiness with the spouse of your choice.

Open yourself up for Uninterrupted Happiness!

BOOKS TO GROW YOU AND YOUR RELATIONSHIP

Books to Build Your Relationship

The 5 Love Languages: The Secret to Love that Lasts; By Gary Chapman

Getting the Love You Want: A Guide for Couples, 20th Anniversary Edition; By Dr. Harville Hendrix

The Seven Principles for Making Marriage Work: A Practical Guide from the Country's Foremost Relationship Expert; By Dr. John Gottman and Nan Silver

Boundaries in Marriage; By Henry Cloud

Mindful Relationship Habits: 25 Practices for Couples to Enhance Intimacy, Nurture Closeness, and Grow a Deeper Connection; By Barrie Davenport and S.J. Scott

Self- Improvement

Success Through Stillness: Meditation Made Simple by Russell Simmons and Chris Morrow

Desperate for Change; By Jacqueline Escalante Deas

ABOUT THE AUTHORS

About Phill

Phill is a successful entrepreneur, business owner and real estate developer. Over the years, he has developed real estate in various areas throughout the country. He is also the owner of a large transportation and logistics corporation that serves the local and state government. Phil has a track record of success with building homes, successful companies, and people. He mentors men who are aspiring real estate investors or business owners and teaches them entrepreneurial skills. As a result of Phill's coaching and mentoring, countless men have built successful and thriving companies. His mentoring and strategies have financially taken many of these men from minimum wage to six-figure incomes!

About Michelle

Michelle, (also known as Motivated Michelle) has impacted thousands of women as an Image and Beauty Consultant. As a veteran entrepreneur for 30 years, Michelle built her business and rose to the top. She is a dynamic public speaker and coach. As a result of her training and ability to connect with women, many have reclaimed and remodeled their lives. Women have applauded her for reaching them in their state of despair and encouraging them to live when they wanted to end it all! In Michelle's business, she discovered how to build women from the inside out. As an image consultant she not only taught them how to look and feel beautiful, she used her spiritual gifts and insight to help these women build confidence and self-esteem, tap into creativity, and see the beauty in themselves. Michelle has taught women how to be successful in network marketing companies. As a result of her coaching, women have repositioned themselves and become financially independent.

Collectively, Phill and Michelle they have a track record of success with building homes, businesses, and people. In Uninterrupted Happiness, Phill and Michelle blend their unique skills to help build and rebuild relationships. Over the years, they have helped many couples. Now, they have synergized with the goal of helping a million people transform themselves and their relationships. Phill and Michelle live in Charlotte, North Carolina.